W9-API-097

RONDA ROUSEY

Champion Mixed Martial Arts Star

Ellina Litmanovich

Enslow Publishing
101 W. 23rd Street
Suite 240
New York, NY 10011
USA

enslow.com

Published in 2018 by Enslow Publishing, LLC.
101 W. 23rd Street, Suite 240, New York, NY 10011

Copyright © 2018 by Enslow Publishing, LLC.

All rights reserved.

No part of this book may be reproduced by any means
without the written permission of the publisher.

Library of Congress Cataloging-in-Publication Data

Names: Litmanovich, Ellina, author.
Title: Ronda Rousey : champion mixed martial arts star / Ellina Litmanovich.
Description: New York, NY : Enslow Publishing, 2018. | Series: Sports Star
  Champions | Includes bibliographical references and index. | Audience:
  Grade 6-8.
Identifiers: LCCN 2017003412| ISBN 9780766086968 (library-bound) | ISBN
  9780766087538 (pbk.) | ISBN 9780766087545 (6-pack)
Subjects: LCSH: Rousey, Ronda—Juvenile literature. | Women martial
  artists—United States—Biography—Juvenile literature.
Classification: LCC GV1113.R69 L57 2018 | DDC 796.8092 [B]—dc23
LC record available at https://lccn.loc.gov/2017003412

Printed in the United States of America

To Our Readers: We have done our best to make sure all websites in this book were active and appropriate when we went to press. However, the author and the publisher have no control over and assume no liability for the material available on those websites or on any websites they may link to. Any comments or suggestions can be sent by email to customerservice@enslow.com.

Photo Credits: Cover, pp. 1, 19 © AP Images; p. 5 The Washington Post/Getty Images; pp. 8, 22, 31, 32 Diamond Images/Getty Images; p. 10 Paul Archuleta/FilmMagic/Getty Images; p. 12 Stephen Dunn/ Getty Images; p. 14 Matthew Stockman/Getty Images; p. 16 Gina Ferazzi/Los Angeles Times/Getty Images; p. 20 Olivier Morin/AFP/Getty Images; p. 21 Toshifumi Kitamura/AFP/Getty Images; p. 25 Frazer Harrison/Getty Images; p. 29 Icon Sports Wire/Getty Images; p. 34 Quinn Rooney/Getty Images; pp. 35, 42 Christian Petersen/Getty Images; p. 38 Taylor Ballantyne/Sports Illustrated/Getty Images; p. 39 Cindy Ord/Getty Images; p. 41 Loic Venance/AFP/Getty Images.

Contents

Introduction:
Rowdy Ronda

How does someone become a champion? How hard would you have to work to become the greatest at the sport that you love? How far would you go to get your body into the best shape possible to survive the endurance of that sport? If you're Ronda Rousey, you'll do everything in your power to make yourself into the best version of who you need to be to win.

For a long time, many of the best fighters within boxing, mixed martial arts (MMA), and Ultimate Fighting Campionship (UFC) have been men. Many of these fighters didn't want women in the ring. It took years for them to be taken seriously in a combat-like sport. Luckily for all, with her wise-cracking jokes and ability to dish it in and out of the ring, Ronda Rousey has become one of the most famous names in the world of UFC.

> **"I'm gonna fight for you someday and I'm going to be your first female UFC world champion."**
> —*Ronda Rousey to Dana White,*
> *president of the UFC*

Ronda Rousey is an actress, an Olympic bronze medalist, and one of the top female MMA fighters in the United States. Rousey is also an advocate for body positivity.

In 2008, Rousey became one of the youngest Americans to win an Olympic medal in the sport of judo. She beat out some of the best Judoka fighters. Rousey had been a top Judoka fighter for most of her teen years and into her early twenties. After her win, between 2008 and 2012, Rousey became more immersed in MMA. In 2012, after a few years of keeping herself out of the spotlight, Rousey won the title of bantamweight champion when she fought Miesha Tate.

Tate had been the reigning MMA bantamweight champion for a long time. No one was able to throw her off her game till she went head-to-head with Rousey. It ended when Rousey dislocated Tate's elbow, causing Tate to succumb to defeat after only 4 minutes and 27 seconds. Rousey became a household name. The fight had been short lived, but that was the moment when everyone wanted to know about Ronda Rousey.

1

Beating the Odds

Ronda Rousey has always been a fighter. Since her first moments of life she has been fighting the world, herself, and all the people around her who do not believe that she possesses the abilities of a fighter or a champion.

Ronda Jean Rousey was born in Riverside, California, on February 1, 1987. She was the third and youngest daughter of AnnMaria De Mars and Ronald Rousey. She was named after her father, Ronald, who had wanted a son. Instead he got Ronda, whom he called Ronnie.

Rousey's first moments of life weren't easy. Her birth had been complicated, and Ronda struggled for breath.

AnnMaria De Mars is not only Ronda Rousey's mother and biggest fan, but she is also a World Judo champion, technology executive, and author.

Ronda's umbilical cord was wrapped around her neck, causing her to lose air. The doctors were able to save her life, but not without complexity.

Ronda's parents were beyond happy that she survived. The doctor who saved Rousey told her parents that she may have brain damage from lack of oxygen. They explained that Ronda would have difficulty in the first few years of life. They were right, but only to an extent.

"Life is a fight from the minute you take your first breath to the moment you exhale your last."

—Ronda Rousey

Ronda developed a little slower verbally than many kids her age. She could not form proper speech due to some damage at birth. For years she struggled with expressing herself through words, but a lot of the time her words came out as mumbles. Rousey tried her best to speak, but nothing came out right.

Ronda didn't let her speech impediment stop her from expressing herself. Ronda's sisters helped her, and eventually she was able to create her own language. The way she expressed herself via speech or arm gestures was the way her family members understood her. Occasionally when no one understood what she wanted, she would break down, kick the person she was talking to if they asked her to repeat herself too many times, or start crying. She didn't cry because her feelings were hurt; she cried because she was frustrated for not being like everyone else.

In the summer of 1990, Rousey's family moved to North Dakota after Ronda's sister Maria saw a shooting in their town of Riverside. AnnMaria and Ron decided it was time to move their family somewhere safer. By this time, Ronda's mother had finished her PhD and had a job offer from Minot State University. The university also offered a great, free speech pathology program for Ronda. It was a no-brainer for the family to move.

North Dakota was completely different from California. The family was able to afford a house on five acres of land. They were surrounded by creeks, trees, and hills. Between the beautiful landscape and speech classes, Ronda was finally able to form her first full sentence.

The first winter in North Dakota was when Ronda's life changed. The day started just like any day in the Rousey family. The hills were covered in snow. Ronda and her sisters were bundled up in warm clothing to go sledding. Their father, Ron, decided to go first to make sure the hill was safe. He went down fast and hit a bump. When he got to the bottom of the hill he couldn't get up. It took an hour for the ambulance to get to her father and even longer to get to the hospital.

After a few surgeries, the family found out that Ron Rousey, Ronda's hero, would never be the same again. His injury was severe. He had a rare bleeding disorder and his spine was

Ronda Rousey, pictured here with her younger sister, Julia De Mars, is very close to her family. All of the Rousey and De Mars women have achieved success in their fields of work.

slowly disintegrating. Although he fought to live for his children, the knowledge of his future demise was too much for him. On August 11, 1995, Ron Rousey took his own life.

Two years after Ron Rousey died, Ronda's mom started dating again. She met Dennis De Mars, a rocket scientist. They married, and in 1998, the Rousey-De Mars clan moved back to California and Ronda's sister Julia was born.

The family moved to Santa Monica, California, close to where one of AnnMaria's friends had a judo club. This was where Rousey began her training about a month before her eleventh birthday. She immediately fell in love with the complexity of the sport. Knowing that you had to figure out your opponent's moves before coming in for the match was something that she enjoyed and found exhilarating.

AnnMaria De Mars

Today she is one of Ronda Rousey's biggest fans, but before Rousey became known to the world as the best female UFC champion, her mother, AnnMaria De Mars, was already known in the sport of judo. In 1984, De Mars was the first American to win a gold medal at the World Judo Championship.

Ronda Rousey (*in blue*) defeats Grace Jividen at the US Olympic trials in 2004. Jividen was a teammate of Rousey's mother, so for Rousey it felt as though she was fighting her mom.

Rousey's first judo fight was on her eleventh birthday. She ended up winning the whole tournament through instant wins, also called *ippons*. The tournament gave her a sense of euphoria. Her second tournament didn't go as well. She won second place. Anastasia's coach, the girl who beat her, told Rousey not to feel bad since Anastasia was a junior national champion. For a moment Rousey felt relieved knowing that she almost beat someone at that level, but then she saw her mother's face. AnnMaria told Ronda that she should never allow herself to be defeated. She should challenge herself, because she can always do better and be the winner. To this day, Rousey feels like she can always do better thanks to her mother.

2

Judoka Master and Olympian

When people hear the term "roughhousing," they usually think of boys fighting each other. Sometimes people say, "Don't worry, boys will be boys." In the Rousey-De Mars house, it was all girls, four to be exact. The girls also had four rules that they needed to follow in the house. To many, these rules would sound ridiculous, but when there are so many kids causing chaos (three that were born in a four-year span) in a household, rules are necessary. One of the rules that the girls had to follow was that you couldn't hit someone unless they hit you first.

Ronda can recall one of the last fights she had with Jennifer, her older sister. She had just started judo but knew

Rousey competes against China's Shumei Dou in the 2004 Titan Games.

she couldn't use the moves she had learned on her sister. That day Jennifer ended up the victor of the fight. Her two older sisters, to this day, say they were the first women to win a fight against the "legendary" Ronda Rousey.

Ronda's first fight outside of the house, but not on the mat, was in sixth grade. A boy who had been bullying Ronda all year decided to come up behind her and choke her. Ronda couldn't breathe. Instead of panicking like most would, she used a judo trick and threw him over her hip and onto the cement. The boy needed stitches and was too embarrassed to complain about the incident.

A few weeks later, another bully decided to fight Ronda. She shoved Ronda a few times, and then Ronda dropped the girl. A school staff member separated the two before it went too far. At first the principal considered suspension, but AnnMaria talked him out of it. She stated that since Ronda didn't start the fight and she didn't really do anything to hurt the girl, she shouldn't be punished. The following day, Ronda was back at school.

What Is Judo?

Judo is a sport that requires great mental and physical prowess. It is derived from the combat sport of jujitsu, which is another method of martial arts. Jujitsu and judo are similar. They both were created for defeating an opponent in close combat. Jujitsu is used to disarm an armed and armored opponent without the use of a weapon. Judo, on the other hand, is close hand-to-hand combat without any weapons, and victory is gained without hurting your opponent. Judo gained its popularity in 1886, when the Tokyo police defeated a popular jujitsu school team. Judo eventually became an Olympic sport in 1964.

One of the things that AnnMaria De Mars taught Rousey was to fight through the pain. At the age of sixteen, Rousey decided to skip school for the first time. She jumped the fence and broke her foot. Instead of raising her hands in defeat, she went

AnnMaria De Mars, the first American to take home the gold at the World Judo Championships in 1984, still enjoys teaching classes in the sport she loves.

to the mall with a throbbing foot. The following day Rousey had a tournament. She beat all of her opponents until the last one. By that time her foot was in so much pain that she had to fight through the pain. Marti Malloy, who eventually became the bronze medalist in judo at the 2012 Olympics, defeated her. After telling her mom the truth about skipping school and losing, Rousey was grounded for a month. Since that moment, Rousey has been fighting through all kinds of injuries.

Rousey's foot still wasn't healed, but she had to keep training. While sparring at Venice Judo, a club in Culver City, her sparring partner crashed into her, crushing her right knee.

At that moment her joint collapsed. She couldn't even get up. Her ACL, a ligament in her knee, was torn. This was one of the worst things an athlete could hear. The surgery would be fast and easy, but the recovery time was at least six months. Ronda was heartbroken.

Ronda had her surgery and started physical therapy a week later. Instead of letting her wallow around and do nothing, AnnMaria made Ronda keep practicing. Rather than put pressure on her knee, Ronda did leg lifts and ab workouts. Two weeks later, her mother took her to a dojo. Until her leg healed, she practiced pins, chokes, and armbars. Her broken knee is the reason why she is now one of the best at armbars. Six months after her surgery, Rousey finished second in the US Open, losing only on points to Sarah Clark. The following week she won the Canadian Open. Her eyes were now set on the Olympics.

After qualifying at the US Open, Ronda became the youngest member qualify for the US national team. There she learned about steroids, banned substances that athletes tend to use. Although many athletes believe that steroids could help them in their sport, Rousey knows that her strength is natural, not man-made, so she does her best to fight with all that she has within.

After the US Open, Ronda knew she would have to get a new coach. Trace Nishiyama had been her coach since she started her training at eleven. She knew that Trace had taught her everything that he could. She also knew that it was time for her to find someone who could take her to the next level.

In 2004 Rousey started training with Jimmy Pedro, aka "Big Jim." Rousey had met Big Jim one month after her surgery. He is the father and coach of "Little Jimmy," the winner of the 1999 world championship. She spent eight months with him in rural New Hampshire. He taught her a lot about discipline. He created a training circuit in his basement. She spent most of her mornings in that basement and her days in his judo club in Massachusetts.

> **"If you can't dream big, ridiculous dreams, what's the point in dreaming at all?"**
> —Ronda Rousey

Rousey had been training for the Olympics since she was six. She started with swimming, but after her father passed, judo became her sport. Rousey qualified for the 2004 Olympics after beating Grace Jividen, one of her mother's friends and competitors, as well as someone twice her age. Rousey came in ninth place at the Olympic Games. She was the best judo competitor on the US Olympic team. She didn't win a medal, but it gave her the determination to do better the next time.

After her defeat in the 2004 Olympics, Rousey trained harder than ever before. A few months later she became the first American to win the junior world championship. Rousey then went to a training camp in Spain Because her "coach" there was no coach, she had to make sure that she was the one watching the competitors and learning their moves.

In early 2005, Rousey had a disagreement with her mother and Big Jim. Between 2005 and 2007, Rousey lived and trained in New York, Chicago, and even in Canada. In 2007, after realizing she was in the wrong and regaining her

Rousey (*in white*) is defeated by Austrian judoka Claudia Heill. Heill went on to win the silver medal at the 2004 Olympics.

self-worth, she returned to train with Big Jim. After 2007, Rousey won multiple championships, including the Austria World Cup. At this event, Rousey finally got her eating habits in order, made a higher weight class, and even beat out girls who were fifteen pounds heavier than those she had fought previously.

Since Rousey's qualifications in 2004, people wondered she could win the Olympics in 2008. Up to that moment no woman from the United States had placed in the Olympics for judo. Rousey had four years of hard training and championships, with her eye on the prize. With many wins and few losses, Rousey was ready.

By defeating Germany's Annett Boehm, Ronda Rousey (*in blue*) won the bronze medal at the 2008 Beijing Olympic Games.

The 2008 Olympics in Beijing, China, had suddenly arrived. Rousey fought hard against her competitors. She beat everyone through tapouts. Then it was Edith Bosch's turn. Rousey had beaten Bosch in the 2007 Rio World Championship. Unfortunately, Bosch had learned Rousey's moves and was able to beat her. This didn't stop Rousey. From that moment she fought even harder against the other opponents. Her last fight was against Annett Böhm, the 2004 Olympic bronze medalist, the person who stood between Rousey and the bronze. Rousey fought with all of her might and came out victorious. Not only had she been the first US female to qualify for the Olympics for judo, but she was now the first to win a medal for America.

3

A Force to Be Reckoned With

Once the Olympics are over, what do you do with yourself? This was the question that Ronda Rousey was contemplating after the 2008 Olympics. She had won the bronze for the United States, and for that they gave her $10,000. That money did not go far. She put it toward a car, but still had a monthly payment. After all of the freedom she had experienced, she knew that she couldn't live at home. Rousey got herself a studio apartment and three jobs just to be able to afford her life.

Ronda Rousey shows off her bronze medal at the 2008 Olympic Games.

After a short break from judo, Ronda Rousey found a new passion, MMA.

Rousey gave herself a year off to live like a "normal" young adult. She wanted to not be responsible. She wanted to eat whatever her heart desired. All of the discipline and training went out the door. Her year of living was not living at all, but a slow torture of figuring out what to do with herself.

After giving herself the year off, Rousey went back full force into training. During her sabbatical, she realized that the bronze medal didn't make her happy and neither did judo. She quit one of her jobs and started a new training regimen. During her first match back since the Olympics, she confided in Little Jimmy, Big Jim's son, about her interest in MMA. He had seen her compete since she was sixteen, so she knew he would understand. She wanted him to be the one to train her in MMA.

Little Jimmy didn't support her decision. She was heartbroken, but it gave her the determination to go out and do it on her own. For weeks she would ask her sparring partner Manny what he thought and what the other guys at the gym thought. Most of them believed that she could beat any woman out there, but to get a coach who would be interested in training a woman in MMA would be difficult.

> **"I'm going to be the one athlete you regret losing for the rest of your life."**
> —Ronda Rousey to Little Jimmy

Another barrier Ronda had to cross was to tell her mother that she wanted to quit judo and train in MMA. Her mother thought it was a terrible idea. To prove herself, Ronda called Darin Harvey and Leo Frincu, her MMA trainers and eventual managers, and the three of them talked to AnnMaria over dinner. They discussed the lack of market for women in the MMA, but they also believed that Rousey had what it takes to become the best at the sport. By the end of the night, after hours of convincing, AnnMaria gave up. She gave Rousey a year to become a top-notch MMA fighter.

It's hard to find a coach when there are few who would want to train you. Rousey had trouble doing just that. In 2010, Rousey started training at the Glendale Fighting Club (GFC), owned by Edmond Tarverdyan. He was an Armenian trainer who had been training fighters since he was sixteen. He was a young guy compared to most trainers in the UFC. At first he saw Rousey as a nuisance who didn't take no for an answer. Each day she would come to the gym and ask him to train her, and every day he would answer her with a no.

After weeks of being denied the same training as her male counterparts, Rousey was furious. She was so fed up with the lack of respect he was showing her that she screamed at him. Her screaming was how she finally got his attention. He had been waiting to make sure that MMA was something she really wanted to do and not just a phase.

Rousey's training at GFC was tough. She spent at least three hours a day hitting the bag, shadowboxing, and doing different drills. Her skills were slowly forming. Tarverdyan sparred with her for less time than the guys, but she took it as a challenge.

Edmond Tarverdyan, Ronda Rousey's coach, is also an Armenian Muay Thai champion.

As her skills developed, Rousey wanted to start fighting in the ring. Her manager would find a girl to fight her, but then the opponent would back out. She finally found someone willing to fight. It was August 6, 2010, and her opponent, Hayden Munoz, was a kickboxer. They got into the ring. Munoz didn't stand a chance. Twenty-three seconds after the referee said "fight," the match was over. This was her debut as an amateur fighter. After another two wins, it was time to turn pro.

What Is MMA?

MMA is a form of mixed martial arts and one of the fastest-growing sports in the world. It takes parts from different disciplines in the world of martial arts, including boxing, kickboxing, karate, tae kwon do, wrestling, and a few other sports. There are usually three rounds of five minutes in each round.

Although MMA is the actual sport, UFC has given the sport most of its popularity. In MMA there are eight weight classes. This gives challengers the same opportunity to win without prejudice of weight. The fighters fight in the "Octagon," which is the name of the cage they are fighting in.

To make ends meet, Rousey was working three jobs. She taught judo to adults, worked for an LA Fitness gym, and had a job at an animal hospital. She was also living with a roommate in an apartment in which most people wouldn't live. Rousey finally lined up a pro fight with Ediane Gomes for March 27, 2011.

Two days before the fight, Rousey heard a commotion in the living room. Her dog and her roommate's dog were fighting. To stop the two from ripping each other apart, Rousey kicked her dog, Mochi. Mochi, still in fight mode, bit Rousey twice in the foot. Instead of panicking, Rousey called her manager.

He sent her to a doctor who was a friend of his. Rousey ended up getting stitches on her arch.

Rousey had been waiting for what felt like months to finally go pro. The doctor told her that she could try to fight, but the stitches could burst and she would have a bad scar. Rousey didn't care. Scar or no scar, she was going to fight. In MMA, if you have stitches, you cannot fight. Rousey distracted the officials during her weigh-in before they noticed there was anything wrong with her foot.

The time had come. It was Gomes vs. Rousey. The undefeated Gomes was 6–0. Although Rousey felt the pain in her foot, she didn't let it stop her for a second. The two women got into the ring, and the fight began. Rousey used her famous move, the armbar, to get Gomes down. Gomes didn't stand a chance. Gomes tapped out after only twenty-five seconds of fighting. Rousey came out victorious! Rousey felt like she was on top of the world. Nothing could feel better.

And then Strikeforce, the highest level of MMA in the women's division, called.

4

From Bantamweight Champion to First Loss

The moment finally came. For months this was what Ronda Rousey had been training for: Strikeforce. The organization was of the highest caliber for women who fought MMA. The organization called to let her know that they were considering her for their roster of fighters. They wanted to see what she could bring to the ring. A fight had been scheduled against Sarah D'Alelio in Las Vegas on August 12, 2011.

D'Alelio, a grappling master, was going to be Rousey's first big fight. It was big enough to be broadcast on Showtime. The day had come when she would finally be paid the big bucks, which would give her more time to train rather than work.

In the first round of their MMA fight, Ronda Rousey (*right*) defeated Sarah D'Alelio via verbal tapout. There was some controversy behind this tapout, but in the end Rousey still received the win.

The fight began. It ended up being controversial. Rousey had put D'Alelio into an armbar. D'Alelio screamed "Ahhh," which is considered a verbal tapout. Within twenty-five seconds of the first round, Rousey beat D'Alelio. Since the tapout was verbal, D'Alelio's fans and commentators "booed" at Rousey. This made her angry, but it also gave her the determination to prove to everyone that she deserved that win.

How do you know that you've made it? If you're Ronda Rousey, it is when you skip over a previous champion who wants the belt back to fight the current champion. After D'Alelio, Rousey knew she had to prove herself. Her next fight was against Julia Budd. Budd had height and arm reach advantage, but Rousey knew she needed the win to go onto the next fight. The fight ended in thirty-nine seconds of the first round.

Ronda Rousey was elated. After the fight with Budd, the Showtime presenter asked Rousey what her plans were. Rousey she said that she was thinking about going down in weight, from 145 pounds (66 kg) to 135 pounds (61 kg)—she wanted to go from women's featherweight down to bantamweight, to beat Miesha Tate and take her title. It was the first time that a woman had made a callout on live television. Technically, her next fight should have been Sarah Kaufman, but the fans wanted a Tate vs. Rousey fight, and that's what they got.

Ronda Rousey was slowly becoming a Strikeforce favorite. Not only was she a pretty face but she was also a force to be reckoned with. Rousey was quick-witted and was starting to gain fans. She was already up in pro wins, four to be exact, but her next step was the prize, the bantamweight championship belt.

Her fight with Tate was scheduled for March 3, 2012. Prior to the fight both Kaufman and Tate expressed their frustration with the outcome. There were rules to follow, and the UFC had gone around those rules. Kaufman also wanted the fight with Tate. She had previously lost her title to the champion, and she wanted it back. But the decision was already made. The fight was on.

Miesha Tate (*left*) and Ronda Rousey face off at the official weigh-in prior to their Strikeforce fight. This fight was a big deal. Rousey's career as a pro MMA fighter began after this match.

"Some people like to call me cocky or arrogant, but I just think, 'How dare you assume I should think less of myself?'"

—Ronda Rousey

Leading to the fight, there were many interviews. Tate didn't believe that Rousey had the ability to beat her. Rousey was too new. She had only one move, the armbar. If Rousey couldn't overpower Tate and get her arm, then what other moves would she even have? Would she be all right with losing? People were starting to talk, with many taking sides. The fight was becoming one of the most talked about matches in women's fighting. The more that people belittled her skills as a fighter, the more Rousey wanted to win.

Tate stood in the red corner, the champion corner. Rousey stood in the blue corner, the challenger corner.

The fight with Tate started off like the others. The rules were set. Both women were giving each other the eye. Tate was a great fighter, but Rousey had been studying her for weeks. Every move that Tate was known for, Rousey learned. Tate did her best to keep her title and even had Rousey in a headlock a few times, but Rousey was just too good. The fight lasted four minutes and twenty-seven seconds.

Ronda Rousey beats Miesha Tate by submission. Rousey used her famous armbar to defeat Tate in less than five minutes.

Miesha Tate

Miesha "Cupcake" Tate was born on August 18, 1986. In high school, Tate joined the all-boys' wrestling team. She was an aggressive competitor, which gave her the chance to win the women's high school championship her senior year. Tate has been fighting in MMA since college.

Tate is a skilled grappler and the reigning UFC women's bantamweight champion. The match between Rousey and Tate in 2012 created the UFC's women's division.

Ronda Rousey was now the bantamweight champion! She had won her fifth fight in a row as well as the belt. She felt unstoppable, but there were those who wanted to challenge her. Rousey's next fight was with Sarah Kaufman. Kaufman was from Victoria, British Columbia. She had been trained in MMA since age seventeen. When she lost her title to Tate, getting that title back was all she wanted. Although she wanted to win the title from Tate herself, Rousey would do. Unfortunately for Kaufman, Rousey beat her in the first round.

Rousey's skills as a fighter opened up the UFC. Dana White, the president of the company, believed that a new women's division should be opened up with no holding back, the same as the men who fought in the ring. In a way, Rousey was an

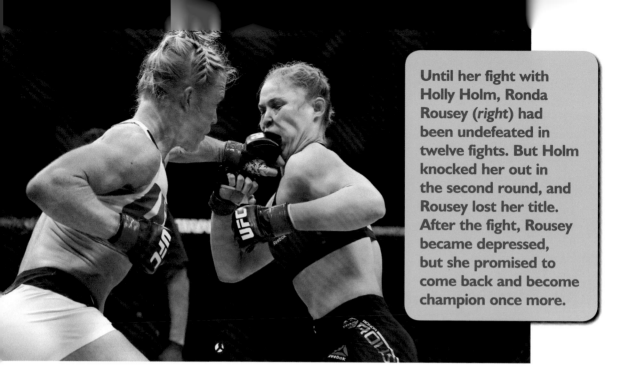

Until her fight with Holly Holm, Ronda Rousey (*right*) had been undefeated in twelve fights. But Holm knocked her out in the second round, and Rousey lost her title. After the fight, Rousey became depressed, but she promised to come back and become champion once more.

innovator. Because of her focus and her determination, she was able to give women this new opportunity to fight.

Ronda Rousey went on to win another six fights, but this time as a UFC fighter. Most of the fights were won through armbar submission, some through knockouts. She went on as undefeated until November 14, 2015, in Melbourne, Australia.

Holly "The Preacher's Daughter" Holm was a good fighter, but she was not considered one of the best. A lot of her wins came from knockouts, but she was still ranked lower than Rousey. Holm had first been a boxing champion; she then became an MMA fighter. Although Rousey had the personality, the passion, and the charisma, Holm was able to beat her through a TKO. Not only was it a TKO, it was in the first round, giving Holm a Guinness World

Record for being the first athlete to hold a world title in both boxing and MMA.

Ronda Rousey lost her very first UFC fight to Holly Holm. In the second round of their match, Holm caught her off guard and knocked Rousey out with a left kick to the head. Through all of the hype surrounding Rousey, the fight had created the highest attendance record since April 2011. After Rousey's defeat, Holm fought Miesha Tate and lost the championship title. Tate then went on to fight Amanda "Cyborg" Nunes but lost to the popular Brazilian fighter.

After a year of training, Rousey came back to the ring. There was a lot of publicity for this fight. Rousey had promised her fans that she would win, but unfortunately that was not the case. Brazil's Amanda Nunes defended her UFC Women's bantamweight championship belt by knocking out Rousey in a short 48 seconds.

The fight between Nunes and Rousey was a big deal. The winner of this fight would be able to call herself the real champion. It was Rousey's first fight since her defeat to Holm, and she wanted the win more than anything. The fight was held in Las Vegas and was featured on pay-per-view with Rousey and Nunes being the main event of the night. Nunes defeated Rousey in 48 seconds by a knockout. Although the fight was supposed to be her redemption, in a statement to ESPN, Rousey said, "Returning to not just fighting, but winning, was my entire focus this past year. However, sometimes—even when you prepare and give everything you have and want something so badly—it doesn't work how you planned. I take pride in seeing how far the women's division has come in the UFC and commend all the other women who have been part of making this possible, including Amanda." Even though Rousey lost the fight, she is still considered one of the best female MMA fighters in the league.

5

Actress, Fighter, and Philanthropist

"I was so happy to have this opportunity because I really do believe that there shouldn't be one cookie cutter body type that everyone is aspiring to be."

—Rousey, Sports Illustrated
behind the scenes video

Ronda Rousey is known to be an outspoken woman. She's usually portrayed as a strong female with a lot of spunk. Although it's been this way for some time now, she wasn't always so self-assured. As a teen, Rousey had been bullied. And even though she could've probably beaten up every person in her school, it still hurt being called names.

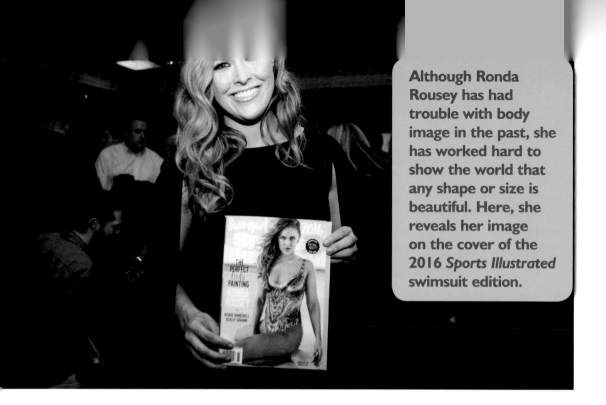

Although Ronda Rousey has had trouble with body image in the past, she has worked hard to show the world that any shape or size is beautiful. Here, she reveals her image on the cover of the 2016 *Sports Illustrated* swimsuit edition.

They made fun of her arms and legs because they were much more muscular than other girls her age. Fighting judo and strength training like she did caused her to have great muscle development.

During her early judo career, Rousey fasted to drop weight for weigh-ins. At one point she was throwing up everything that she ate. To show girls that being healthy is better than living life constantly thinking about weight, she decided to have a charity event at the Glendale Fighting Club, the ring where she trains. It was a two-hour learning session hosted by Rousey where she taught MMA and judo to thirty people.

Today, she wants to show girls of all ages and sizes that they shouldn't feel bad for not having the "perfect" body.

No one has a perfect body. Every woman is different and she should be proud of it. Rousey wants girls to realize that some are skinny and others are curvy, but each girl is beautiful in her own way. In March 2016, Rousey and her mother hosted the Reebok Women's Luncheon. The luncheon showcased the commitment that Reebok has in pushing boundaries and celebrating inspirational women. The hashtag that they used was #PerfectNever, which was actually perfect for the occasion.

Reebok Women asked Ronda Rousey to be their spokeswoman for the 2016 #PerfectNever campaign. As someone who has learned to love her body and wants to throw positivity out into the world, Rousey was a great success in her role.

EA Sports

Rousey was asked to be part of the EA Sports UFC 2 video game. She's even on the cover with UFC featherweight champion Conor McGregor. As a video game fan, she enjoyed seeing how everything was created, but she said she wouldn't use herself in the game. "It weirds me out to see myself and play as myself."

Rousey had also created T-shirts through the website Represent. Represent creates merchandise for celebrities and non-celebrities alike to help raise money for charity. All of the proceeds go to Didi Hirsch Mental Health Services, which helps women who have difficulty with body image. Her goal is to raise money for those suffering with body negativity.

Another two charities that Rousey donates to are called The Shade Tree and Noah's Animal House. The Shade Tree is a shelter for women in Las Vegas and Noah's Animal House provides refuge for the animals of abused women. This way the women can stay with their animals without having to leave them behind.

Rousey isn't letting fame get to her head, but she's enjoying the ride. She has had a few small roles in movies. One of the more famous was *Furious 7*. Rousey played a villainous role, but she had the privilege to fight Michelle Rodriguez. The fight scene showed that women could fight just as well as men in the movies. She also became close to Vin Diesel. After taping a scene, they would both play World of Warcraft.

Rousey has also been in *The Expendables 3* and *Entourage*, where she fights the character Turtle after he asks her on a date. Those who have worked with her on set said that she is one of the funniest and most professional people to work with. She has a few other movies coming out, but for now her concentration is on fighting and winning. Although she has been on multiple talk shows and has met many celebrities, she feels like all of this is a dream that can be taken away.

Ronda Rousey is working on a career as an actress. Here, she poses with her castmates from the movie *The Expendables 3*.

Ronda Rousey is a strong female inside and out, and that is why many young women look up to her. No matter whether she wins or loses in the future, she has already made a huge impact on the world of MMA and the lives of women of all shapes and sizes.

Rousey also has plenty of endorsements. She understands that there is a dark side to fame, but sometimes there is some good that can come from it. In December 2016, Rousey partnered up with Pantene hair products on a campaign called "Strong is Beautiful" to show that strong women can be just as beautiful as any other woman. She is a great source of empowerment to young girls everywhere. In an interview with *Vogue* magazine Rousey said, "A lot of women out there are just naturally thin, and that doesn't mean that they're not strong in their own ways. Strength is more than just what's physical."

Ronda Rousey is a strong woman, a businesswoman, and a role model to girls everywhere. No matter where her journey takes her, she will always be known as one of the best MMA fighters of all times. As Dana White stated, "She's a beast, man. She's the greatest athlete I've ever worked with. With her, it's like the Tyson era, like, how fast is she gonna destroy somebody, and in what manner? Ronda's one in a million."

UFC Career and Stats

RONDA ROUSEY'S OFFICIAL PROFESSIONAL MMA FIGHT RECORD

Date	Result	Opponent	Event
12/30/2016	Loss	Amanda Nunes	UFC 207: Nunes vs. Rousey
11/14/2015	Loss	Holly Holm	UFC 193: Rousey vs. Holm
08/01/2015	Win	Bethe Correia	UFC 190: Rousey vs. Correia
02/28/2015	Win	Cat Zingano	UFC 184: Rousey vs. Zingano
07/05/2014	Win	Alexis Davis	UFC 175: Weidman vs. Machida
02/22/2014	Win	Sara McMann	UFC 170: Rousey vs. McMann
12/28/2013	Win	Miesha Tate	UFC 168: Weidman vs. Silva
02/23/2013	Win	Liz Carmouche	UFC 157: Rousey vs. Carmouche
08/18/2012	Win	Sarah Kaufman	Strikeforce: Rousey vs. Kaufman
03/03/2012	Win	Miesha Tate	Strikeforce: Tate vs. Rousey
11/18/2011	Win	Julia Budd	Strikeforce 11/18/11
08/12/2011	Win	Sarah D'Alelio	Strikeforce Challengers
06/17/2011	Win	Charmaine Tweet	School of Hard Knocks 12
03/27/2011	Win	Ediane Gomes	King of the Cage: Turning Point

RONDA ROUSEY'S AMATEUR MMA FIGHT RECORD

Date	Result	Opponent	Event
01/07/2011	Win	Taylor Stratford	The Future Stars of MMA!
11/12/2010	Win	Autumn Richardson	The Future Stars of Mixed Martial Arts

Chronology

February 1, 1987 Ronda Rousey is born in Riverside, California.

1990 The Rousey family moves to Minot, North Dakota; Ronda starts speech therapy.

Winter 1990 Ron Rousey hurts himself during a sledding accident. This accident changes Ronda's life.

1991 The family relocates to Jamestown, North Dakota.

August 1995 Ron Rousey passes away.

March 1998 AnnMaria marries a "rocket scientist" named Dennis De Mars. They have a daughter named Julia, AnnMaria's fourth daughter, but first with Dennis.

1999 Ronda starts training in judo.

2002 Ronda, at the young age of fifteen, qualifies for the US Olympic team.

2003 At the age of sixteen becomes the youngest American to rank No. 1 in the women's half-middleweight division.

2004 Wins the gold medal at the World Junior and Pan American Judo Championships.

2007 Wins the silver medal in World Judo Championships, bronze medal in German Open, gold medal in Pan American Games, and bronze medal in Pan American Championships in judo.

2008 Takes home the bronze medal at the Olympics after beating Annett Böhm of Germany.

2010 Makes her amateur MMA debut by beating Hayden Munoz within 23 seconds.

2011 Makes her pro MMA debut at the King of the Cage: Turning Point; defeats Ediane Gomes in 25 seconds.

2011 Makes her Strikeforce debut against Sarah D'Alelio; defeats D'Alelio in the first round by technical submission due to an armbar.

2012 Becomes the Strikeforce women's bantamweight champion by defeating Miesha Tate.

December 2013 Defends her UFC title against Miesha Tate in a rematch; defends her title by beating Sarah Kaufman at Strikeforce in 54 seconds.

2014 Defends her title again after being challenged by Alexis Davis at UFC 175. She won the fight in the first round via knockout, after only 16 seconds of fighting.

August 2014 Appears in *The Expendables 3*.

2015 Makes an appearance in the films *Furious 7* (April) and *Entourage* (May).

November 2015 Loses first fight of her UFC career as well as her title of bantamweight champion to Holly Holm.

December 2016 Loses against Amanda "Cyborg" Nunes.

Glossary

armbar A common submission hold in which an opponent's arm is straightened out between the instigator's thighs, before being bent and hyperextended at the elbow to the point of submission.

boxing A combat sport and form of striking where only the knuckles of the padded glove are used to strike the head and upper torso of an opponent.

dojo A room or hall in which judo and other martial arts are practiced.

grappling A general term that covers the techniques and disciplines used to gain an advantage over an opponent without the use of striking.

kickboxing The generic term for a sport and style of striking that utilizes hand and foot techniques.

knockout A strike that leaves an opponent unable to continue and results in a premature conclusion to a bout.

referee An official appointed by the applicable athletic commission and someone fully responsible for ensuring the bout rules are adhered to and that the safety of the athletes is paramount.

round A five-minute time period within which two fighters compete under mixed martial arts rules. Non-title bouts consist of three rounds and title fights consist of five rounds.

submission The result of a grappling technique that forces an opponent to concede defeat via tapout or other means.

tapout The act of a struggling competitor signaling to the referee, usually by quickly tapping three times on the mat or opponent, that he or she gives up and concedes defeat.

Further Reading

Books

Gitlin, Marty. *Martial Arts and Their Greatest Fighters.* New York, NY: Rosen Publishing, 2015.

Harmon, Daniel E. *Grappling and Submission Grappling.* New York, NY: Rosen Publishing, 2013.

Rousey, Ronda. *My Fight/Your Fight.* New York, NY: Regan Arts, 2015.

Straka, Mike. *Rowdy Rousey: Ronda Rousey's Fight to the Top.* New York, NY: Triumph Books, 2015.

Websites

Ronda Rousey Official Site
www.rondarousey.net
This is an official site run by Ronda Rousey's team. You can find information about her stats as a fighter and updates on her life.

"Rowdy" Ronda Rousey—Official UFC® Fighter Profile
www.ufc.com/fighter/Ronda-Rousey?id=
This site has news and statistics of Rousey's fights. It is also the main site of the UFC.

Index